I0060522

THE
GROUND
FLOOR

**THE CASE FOR TRANSPARENCY,
ACCOUNTABILITY, AND SERVICE
IN COMMERCIAL REAL ESTATE**

KEVIN SAXE

THE GROUND FLOOR
*The Case for Transparency,
Accountability, and Service in
Commercial Real Estate*

ISBN 978-1-61961-312-6

LIONCREST
PUBLISHING

CONTENTS

CHECK OUT THE GROUND FLOOR BLOG

The Ground Floor is more than
just a book. It's online too.

The Ground Floor Blog is the best place for
up to date wisdom on the commercial real
estate industry. It's focused on connecting my
own experiences as a service provider with
principles from modern studies and authors
with the intention of progressing transparency
and authenticity in commercial real estate.

Simply, the mission of the blog is to catalog my
thoughts on how we may serve others, create
value through outward thinking, and grow
ourselves and our businesses in the process.

You can find more at:

www.thegroundfloor.co

1

THE PROBLEM

I MADE MY FORAY INTO REAL ESTATE WHEN I
was 22 years old and fresh out of college. Real estate
was something that had always kind of appealed to
me; it was tangible, whereas so many of the jobs my
friends were moving into seemed to be built on air.
Markets were malleable, finance was just numbers
on a screen, consulting was...whatever the consul-
tant said it was. A building, on the other hand, was
a real thing; the offices inside were priced at a cost
per square foot, and that cost was held accountable
to the costs of the other spaces in the same building.
It was straightforward. There was room for creativity

and negotiation but not for BS. At least, that's what I thought.

I was hired by a Fortune 1000 real estate firm and placed squarely into a role befitting a recent graduate, which is to say that I was up to my neck in paper. As an analyst to the office brokers, I began to better understand the real estate space, including the real estate investment space. I liked it well enough, but I knew I didn't want to stay there. For my friends, however, finance was the industry of choice. A lot of my college friends, who were, at that time, the bulk of my network, were immersed in investment banking in some way, shape, or form, and though it wasn't the career I wanted for myself, it was something I had an interest in. Finance talk was what comprised most of our happy hours (at least for the first round of beers), and even though I wasn't working in the same capacity as they were, I had always been pretty good with numbers. It could be a challenge, but I managed to keep pace with even their most complex conversations—at least most of the time. Finance and numbers were just something I understood. Little did I know the kind of impact those conversations would later have on my professional life.

However, my time in an analyst role was short-lived; I quickly moved into the tenant representation side of my firm. It was a relatively older, very experienced department that comprised sales professionals selling to the highest levels—CEOs, CFOs, and others with impressive titles. I was one of the few young guys walking around the floor and probably would have been really intimidated by that environment if I didn't have that thick layer of unawareness that most guys in their early twenties have, making me impervious to the pressure. My new job was to help my clients find a commercial office space that met their needs and then negotiate the office lease transactions; this process could be incredibly difficult for anyone who didn't deal with commercial real estate professionally. I knew it was a straightforward yet important role and one that was very necessary in a surprisingly complicated industry.

When a company needs to buy an office building or find office space to lease, it's easier said than done. Finding a space is time-consuming, and when you do finally find the one you want, it often comes with an affiliated broker who will hand over a massive lease and expect you to figure out how to navigate all the ins and outs of the document (and there are *a lot* of ins and outs; most commercial leases are over 50 pages long). But the broker affiliated with the building works *for the owner—the landlord*. The broker is a third-party leasing agent hired specifically to market the property and then help the owner achieve the highest rate possible (and the most contractual protection possible). Simply put, they're not on *your* side—they're looking out for the building's owner.

Tenant reps, on the other hand, are on your side and have the expertise and market familiarity to make the process so much easier. They will save you time and fight for your best interests. In my new role, I was helping clients identify the opportunities available to them, and after they found a few they liked, I would negotiate the deal, often by pitting the properties against one another to try to bring the cost per square foot down. In that way, the industry serves as a very necessary exchange forum, much like Wall Street. (Despite discrepancies, Wall Street fuels the economy through mutually beneficial exchanges ranging from raising capital for firms through stock, investors aiding banks to fund the debt market, and consultation on how to invest personal or company capital.) We represent those who do not have the expertise to find office space and negotiate leases and those who wouldn't have the time for it even if they did. Our Houston-based clientele mainly run oil and gas companies; they don't know the slightest thing about how much they should be paying on an office lease. And with tenant brokers in place, they don't have to. It is a job that requires relationship building and trust. It also added another tangible element to my job—helping people. I loved it.

The industry serves a great need, but as I soon found out, it doesn't work in the way you might expect.

One of the first "big" transactions I did as a tenant rep broker was with the vice chairman of my company—a man at the highest level of the business. We negotiated a lease together on behalf of a group, and I thought we were doing a great job. I was getting to work with one of the top guys in the field, and I was holding my own. We closed the deal, and it was the first big amount of money I had ever made. I was thrilled. Later, through nothing more than an overheard conversation, I found out that another deal was done in the same building around the same time for a much lower cost per square foot. We had been skinned and had no idea. We thought we had brought the owners down as low as they would go! We certainly had no reason to think that we had missed the mark by as much as we had. We had walked out of negotiations happy, and more importantly, our clients had been extremely happy. It's unlikely we would have ever even found out the difference if it hadn't been for a random snippet of conversation. It ate at me. How could we have been that off the mark? I finally walked up to the vice chairman's office and told him what I'd learned. He didn't look happy at the news, but he didn't look surprised either.

"How does this happen?" I asked.

He had nothing to offer except his interpretation of the market and the reassurance that it was not my fault. "Well, we didn't get a very great deal, but that doesn't happen every time. It's just a risk we run."

I walked out of his office wondering exactly what we were offering our clients. I knew that we created a lot of value; we helped negotiate lease terms, dealt with insurance provisions, and I knew we had gotten a better deal than anything our clients could negotiate on their own. But I had a hard time wrapping my head around the fact that the industry that I believed was concrete and straightforward was, in fact, the complete opposite. It now felt to me like the value we provided was mostly intangible in an industry that was so opaque that even the biggest deal of my career to date felt like little more than broker versus broker. The industry that I had chosen because it felt "real" to me was anything but; I was dealing in air. The market was so shrouded—built so heavily in favor of the other side—that I felt like I was playing high-stakes poker against someone who never had to show their hand.

I couldn't believe that I was the only person who seemed to feel this way (I would later find out that I was not the only one). Still, the vice chairman, a man at the highest level of my company, hadn't batted an eyelash over what I'd considered a failed deal. It was just the way the job worked. After all of his years of experience and success in the industry, he felt that *things are done because that's the way they've always been done* was a sufficient answer; it made sense to him. It made sense to the other tenant rep brokers around me, who saw no reason to question the competitive system, the lack of transparency, the lack of accountability, or the fact that our client-based service was built on a sales model. Somehow, it all made sense within that sales model—the one that wanted us to have relationships with our clients but not necessarily serve them. *Sometimes we get a good deal, and sometimes we don't.*

It just didn't make any sense to me.

2

THE IMPORTANCE OF TRANSPARENCY & ACCOUNTABILITY

IMAGINE YOU ARE A BUSINESS OWNER WHO has seen some success and are now moving out of your garage and into your first commercial space. You sign a lease for five years that will cost you a total of $5 million—a major cost, given that you're still growing—and then you later find out that your neighbor moved in at the exact same time but was only paying $3.8 million for the same size and style space. You had trusted your tenant rep when he'd told you that you had walked away with a great deal when, in reality, you were paying an extra million dollars—money that could have been used to further grow and advance your business at this crucial stage. How would you feel?

When I imagine this scenario, "outraged" doesn't begin to cover it.

Yet, gaps this big can (and do) exist within the same building all the time. Rent discrepancies range more than 40%, with no system in place to keep them in check. The normal market forces that would bring prices to equilibrium don't exist because the information that would make that possible isn't available publicly. The owners of commercial real estate properties intentionally keep the data confidential; this way, they can manipulate each transaction to achieve the highest possible return on their investment.

The problem stems from how the industry itself is set up. The law is on the side of the owners and landlords; they are allowed to keep their information secret, by including confidentiality provisions in their lease terms to prevent the spread of information or the creation of a central database (like the kind that exists in residential real estate), and to set their rates at whatever they want. The tenant rep side is flawed too. It's a sales industry with professionals working for large firms but essentially working as independent contractors looking out for their own gain. And because each rep is looking out for his individual self-interest, he sees his coworkers as competitors instead of collaborators and keeps his information to himself.

These problems could all be improved (if not solved) by an industry-wide increase in transparency and accountability. Unfortunately, these two things are very rare in the commercial real estate industry.

The lack of transparency and accountability within the traditional tenant rep industry is astonishing. It derives from a number of sources and from both sides of the negotiation table. In my belief, the traditional system is broken inside and out.

So how does this happen?

If you are an executive—or have been charged with selecting a new commercial space for your business—perhaps this will ring a bell: When local companies come to a commercial real estate firm, I have to imagine that their assumption is that what I do for a living is similar to what a residential real estate professional does. And why wouldn't they? The comparison would make a lot of sense. When someone is trying to buy a home, it's very easy to navigate the market because everything is really transparent. All the information you would need to make an informed decision is available either within the industry or on a public forum or database.

Your residential real estate broker knows how much the house next door sold for, he knows how much the house down the street sold for, and he can use that knowledge to help you make your offer with excellent assurance that you're getting fair market value. There are also a number of public forums and databases that a potential homeowner or renter can use to find property, compare rates, and know how the value of one property compares to another. Whether they've rented an apartment in college, bought their first condo, or bought their third vacation home, everyone has some level of familiarity with residential real estate. Therefore, it is perfectly logical for them to assume that commercial real estate would work in the same way.

In actuality, however, tenant rep brokerage in commercial real estate is very, very different than it is in the residential market.

For one thing, the way commercial real estate firms operate internally is very different from the operations of residential firms. My clients often assumed that they were getting access to the entire company's knowledge and experience base and that the team of reps would share information amongst each other to fill in any knowledge gaps. How could they know that we were actually working as independent contractors? My clients only got me. And given the individualized nature of the role, there is very little incentive for traditional tenant rep brokers to share their information with anyone else. And my job was made a lot more difficult because of a surprising lack of information.

When companies hire a broker at one of these traditional firms, the expectation is that the broker will know the market through and through—that, like a residential real estate agent, they will know (or be able to look up) the ballpark market value of any given commercial space. I've driven through Houston with clients who have pointed out the window at a random building and said, "What did that building actually lease for recently?" In commercial real estate, questions such as that one are very difficult to answer (other than giving the information the landlord advertises) with a high degree of certainty, because that information is not available publicly; there is no

Zillow for the commercial real estate market. Yes, there is pricing information available, but we can only see what the owner or landlord is *asking* for the property—not what spaces are actually selling for.

Answering those questions is made even more difficult by the volume of commercial property that is available. There are 200 million square feet of commercial real estate in Houston, TX, and the average broker might do only 20 to 30 transactions a year. Even the best broker in the business cannot possibly know the value of more than a small percentage of spaces—and that's only *if* those prices remain static from year to year, which they don't. The best tenant rep broker in the world would, at best, be able to offer an educated guess.

In traditional tenant rep brokerage, the only way clients can know whether they received a good deal or not is based on the subjective opinion of the rep who brokered the deal. There's the rub. Without any transparency in the industry and no database to log into to check for discrepancies between what the asking price is and what the spaces around it are actually leasing for, most tenant rep brokers can't give their clients a definitive *yes* that can be backed by actual numbers. Two tenants, represented by two different but equally good brokers, can each negotiate an office lease in the same building at the same time, and one of them might end up paying 30% more for the space. And when you're talking about commercial real estate, that difference could be hundreds of thousands—if not millions—of dollars. Yet, in both transactions, each client and broker would walk away thinking that they had received the best deal, even though one of them drastically overpaid. It happens all the time, but no one seems to know any better. The broker believes he did the best he could for his client with the information available to him; the client believes the broker is working in a transparent market.

NET EFFECTIVE DEAL

6 MONTH PERIOD

Tenant	Net Effective Deal	Date
TENANT 1	$14	MAY 2009
TENANT 2	$11	JUN 2009
TENANT 3	$15	AUG 2009
TENANT 4	$16	AUG 2009
TENANT 5	$16	SEP 2009
TENANT 6	$10	SEP 2009
TENANT 7	$12	OCT 2009
TENANT 8	$12	NOV 2009
TENANT 9	$14.50	NOV 2009

12 MONTH PERIOD

TENANT 1	$27	MAR 2009
TENANT 2	$18.00	APR 2009
TENANT 3	$22.50	AUG 2010
TENANT 4	$22.50	NOV 2010
TENANT 5	$21.00	DEC 2010
TENANT 6	$22.00	DEC 2010
TENANT 7	$23.50	DEC 2010

12 MONTH PERIOD

TENANT 1	$16.50	AUG 2011
TENANT 2	$18.50	SEP 2011
TENANT 3	$18.00	NOV 2011
TENANT 4	$17.50	NOV 2012
TENANT 5	$20.50	MAY 2012

12 MONTH PERIOD

Tenant	Net Effective	Date
TENANT 1	$19.64	MAY 2011
TENANT 2	$17.00	JUL 2011
TENANT 3	$18.00	FEB 2012
TENANT 4	$19.50	MAR 2012
TENANT 5	$18.00	AUG 2012

The lack of transparency in the market is so counter-intuitive that our clients never even think to ask us how we know for sure, or if we can concretely demonstrate with real figures, that they got a fair deal. And the fact is, sometimes clients don't get the best deal, and the odds are that neither they nor their rep will ever know.

It's just the nature of the business—the way things work—and no one really questions it.

I certainly didn't.

The internal issues were the most unexpected for me. Before entering the industry, I presumed that I would be working with a team of coworkers and that the culture of the company would be collaborative and supportive. I learned very quickly that the tenant rep is essentially an independent entrepreneur. So, even though I was working within a big company, I was essentially working only for myself. Individual reps are responsible solely for their own numbers, motivation, and most surprisingly, their own sources of information. I was shocked by how little collaboration there was between the other reps and me, even if we were working on two separate spaces in the same building! I didn't question it too much, though. I was one of the youngest and newest to the field: I was juggling learning the ropes with attempting to make a respectable name for myself within the company and the industry.

It made no sense to me that we didn't operate under a client-first model; instead, it was a sales model. *We* were the commodities. We were selling our clients on us, and on our ability to land the best deal, rather than the deal itself. "I have more experience than my competitors." "I've done more transactions in this submarket." "I've done more transactions in this building." And while those statements may be true, a really good broker still only does 20 to 30 transactions a year—to put it simply, 15 to 20 transactions a year in a city with over 10 submarkets, dozens of buildings per submarket, and 200 million square feet of office space alone. It is only likely that a broker has done a couple of transactions in your particular submarket and, therefore, highly unlikely that he has done a deal in your building. Furthermore, even if he has done a deal in your particular building, it might have been done at a different time (even years ago) and in an industry dominated by the ever-changing "market"; that information does little to move the needle for your particular transaction. We were the commodities, so we allowed our clients to believe that deals done in a submarket or experience translated directly to the tangible economic worth of a tenant's space. We went along easily with the preexisting notion that our clients have about our information being based in cold, hard numbers, but in reality, very little is. Clients never seemed to think to ask otherwise, and brokers never seemed to question why the industry was run in such an opaque way.

This isn't to say that a small circle of people are working in the shadows to manipulate the industry; it's just that the tenant brokerage side doesn't have much control over their fate. Those on the other side of the table—the owners and landlords—are highly incentivized to keep their information to themselves. To negotiate effectively, we need three different components: market, financial underwriting of the asset, and comparable comps. The owners and landlords control all the information with a tight fist, allowing tenant reps access to only one-third of the information we actually need to negotiate. Essentially, owners and landlords are approaching the table with a very sophisticated advantage, and as tenant rep brokers, we are armed with nothing more than our knowledge of the market and the advertised information that the landlords provide. The opacity of the commercial market allows them to get the highest returns on their buildings. If they can negotiate a million-dollar contract instead of a $750,000 contract, they're going to do it. More than that, the owners of these office buildings put confidentiality provisions in every single lease so that the information *can't* be put into a central database. And they are legally enabled to do so because the law is on the side of the owners. It says that they don't have to give anyone—not even the brokers working for them—more information than the specific data that is being negotiated, which is simply the asking price (not the actual market value). Unless a broker already has a tenant in the building, he won't know how much is being paid for the space inside. And if he does know, he's not going to share his information with the other people in his company; he's going to keep it to himself. My coworkers were my biggest competitors, and in typical tenant rep mode, I, too, kept all of my data and information under lock and key rather than sharing it with the guy on the other side of the wall. If I gave away my information, I'd be giving away my edge.

To put it simply, both sides bear responsibility for the complete lack of transparency in the commercial real estate industry. The owners and landlords are incentivized to not share their information with the tenant reps on the other side of the table. Traditional tenant reps are incentivized to not share their information with the tenant reps on the other side of the room. So everyone—reps and their clients—stay in the dark.

And with that lack of transparency comes a real lack of accountability on both sides. The owners and landlords are able to enter into negotiations holding all the cards. They are not held to the "market" (market being unknown and fluid), nor are they bound to keep their pricing within the range of fair market value. They are accountable only to their investors' desired rate of return. The opacity of the industry is very favorable to them—and is one that they benefit from greatly—and they have no desire to see it change.

In their own way, tenant reps also benefit from the lack of transparency. By virtue of the fact that so much of what tenant reps do is unseen and unknown by both the client and even the person sitting in the desk next to ours, there is a lot of autonomy and very little accountability. In their efforts to sign new clients, tenant reps in traditional firms can make a lot of claims without having to bother with a tangible follow-through. They don't need to prove that they can deliver what they're promising, because no one asks them to.

In this way, you get a lot of "experts." The people in my profession claim to be experts at everything. A typical pitch usually consists of claiming high-level analytical expertise, followed by a demonstration—"I'm going to run this analysis for you"—before running a simple cash flow analysis. Then comes "I grind through the lease document better than anybody"; so now they're professing legal expertise. It all culminates with, "And what if your space was more efficient?" *Wow, are you an architect too?* It reminds me of what one top-performing tenant rep broker said when asked why he loved his job:

> *What I love about it is that it's a little bit of everything. You're a salesman, a consultant, a bit of an attorney, part construction guy, and a big problem-solver and strategic thinker. You're also a space planner, a bit of an architect, and a financial analyst or accountant.*

That is an easy claim to make when you don't have to actually prove your expertise in any of those fields. I could be an expert at five different things because I didn't have to actually *be* an expert; my "expertise" was never put to the test. I never had to tell a client, "This is how I did it, and here are the comparable results," because they never asked me to. All they got was a statement from us saying, "I saved you one million." But one million compared to what? It isn't right; if you're promising expertise, then you need to actually be able to provide it. The (unproven but truly believed) ability to make claims of expertise as a selling tactic to land more business—because that's really what it is—is one way that tenant reps benefit from this opaque industry.

"You can't manage what you can't measure," is a popular adage that has made the rounds through every business conference and managerial summit out there—and with good reason. If you don't keep track of the numbers—the *actual data* of what is going on within your company and your industry—you will never have a clear picture of what is working, what isn't, or whether it's time to make a big change. Companies that do measure these important figures are able to see what their employees are doing, understand how their business is faring, and most importantly, determine whether their clients are actually receiving what they have been promised. With measurement comes transparency, and with transparency comes accountability. If something isn't working, the numbers will show the need for change, allowing the issue to then be better managed.

I've seen this in action, and I know firsthand how effective it is in holding a company and its employees accountable. Although it felt like I was the only one questioning the lack of accountability, many sophisticated real estate users were starting to demand more. I was working for a massively successful global company that is a leader in its industry and in business at large. This company prized transparency and accountability as one of the key facets of how the business was managed. As a rep, I was required to keep data on every transaction I made—almost like keeping a scorecard—collecting enough information to hold myself accountable at every step of every deal I was involved in. With that kind of visibility (and the personal responsibility that came with it), I was committed to serving my client the *right* way. The way the business was managed left a lasting impression on me. The culture of transparency held us accountable to truly *serving* our clients in a way they could verify. In other words, the transparency and accountability demanded by our clients raised the standard of what we, in turn, delivered. Transparency, therefore, led to greater service. That service-oriented perspective has stuck with me to this day and is a shift that I truly believe the commercial real estate industry, as a whole, eventually needs to make.

A new perspective—one that prioritizes serving our clients by being accountable to them—would do wonders for building relationships with our clients. It would shift the tenant rep's focus from his individual success (which is where the sales model on which this industry is built tells him to focus) to truly putting his client first and having the numbers to prove that he's done so. When the focus is on the client, rather than the broker, it goes a long way toward strengthening the relationship in a way that benefits both sides. In *Winning with People,* I love how John Maxwell describes this simple but important notion of putting others first:

> *Two great prime ministers in Great Britain's history are William Gladstone and Benjamin Disraeli. It's said that a young lady went to dinner with them on successive nights. When asked for her impressions of the two men, she said, "When I left the dining room after sitting next to Mr. Gladstone, I thought he was the cleverest man in England. But after sitting next to Mr. Disraeli, I thought I was the cleverest woman in England!"*

It should come as no surprise which prime minister the young woman preferred.

For a relationship-based industry, there is a surprising lack of priority placed on how the client feels. Actually *serving* the client is not an industry-wide part of the culture, because traditional tenant rep brokerage is not built on a service model; it's about slamming a deal home. That's not necessarily a terrible thing, provided that clients aren't unhappy and no one is being mistreated; after all, a service model isn't what the client is expecting. The woman in the story still liked William Gladstone.

A service model is a mindset as much as it is a model; it is a conscious decision to prioritize the needs, desires, and interests of your client before your own bottom line. It's a choice to care more about your client than you do for your own end of the bargain. But isn't that what a service provider is supposed to be? Transparency, accountability, and a visible commitment to service are the best ways to take action toward making that change. And while that choice pays off in ways that may not be readily apparent to those who are comfortable in their status quo, the impact on the success of the business can be huge.

In *Lead with a Story: A Guide to Crafting Business Narratives that Captivate, Convince, and Inspire,* Paul Smith illustrates perfectly the importance of prioritizing and being held accountable to the customer experience (and the benefits of doing so) with the story of Sue Soldo's trip to a popular bed-and-breakfast in Sedona, Arizona. She had chosen to stay at the Adobe Grand Villas because the property had an extraordinary reputation for its customer service, and having just finished chemotherapy treatment for breast cancer, it sounded like the perfect place to unwind. Upon her return from her trip, however, Sue realized that she had left her custom-fit (and super-expensive) mouth guard in her room at the bed-and-breakfast. Smith continues:

> In desperation, she called Adobe. They were apologetic and empathetic but didn't offer much hope. 'It could be anywhere in the dumpster by now.' Sue hung up knowing that she would never see that mouth guard again, and that a $500 trip to the dentist was in her future.
>
> Three days later, however, a small package arrived in the mail from Sedona. Tanya, the innkeeper at Adobe, found the mouth guard! She had to wallow in the dumpster up to her hips to find and return the missing treasure.

After an incredible story like that, it should come as no surprise to learn that Sue became a customer of that inn for life. Dumpster diving is a level of customer service that few people are likely to forget. Was Sue expecting someone from the property to drop what they were doing to hunt for her mouth guard? Of course not! It never even occurred to her to ask. She hung up the phone, still feeling positive about her stay; she certainly hadn't been mistreated, and her relaxing weekend in Sedona had met all of her expectations. However, the innkeeper of the Adobe

Grand Villas had wanted to make her *feel better*; she'd felt accountable to maintaining the standard of customer service that the resort was known for. She prioritized her customer's experience over her bottom line and was willing to give up some of her own time to endure some short-term discomfort (standing waste-deep in garbage definitely counts) to surpass Sue's expectations.

This is a shift in perspective that would benefit the tenant rep industry so much. By virtue of the accountability built into the resort's internal culture, the innkeeper felt personally responsible for maintaining the high standard of customer satisfaction and, as a result, took extra steps to secure Sue's happiness without a second thought. It's a demonstration of true relationship building and service and one that paid off for the Adobe Grand Villas when Sue later wrote a glowing review on Tripadvisor.com, detailing the story of her stellar customer service experience.

Smith concludes the story:

> But the benefit of Sue's story goes beyond its marketing value. Just as it shows potential guests what they have to look forward to, it shows the staff at Adobe what's expected of them. That, in turn, leads to more unparalleled service, which leads

to other pleased guests leaving their own stories,
starting the whole cycle again.

The benefit of accountability, customer prioritization, and a business model so dedicated to service was apparent both externally and internally at the Adobe Grand Villas. It told existing and future customers that these were people whom they could trust; it told the employees that they were expected to be people whom the customers could trust. And in a business that relies on the trust of its customers—whether it is a bed-and-breakfast or a commercial real estate firm—this kind of impact cannot be discounted. The current lack of transparency and accountability in the commercial real estate industry is a problem. The owners and landlords are held to almost no account at all; they are allowed to work in the shadows, controlling all the available information and never having to show their cards. Tenant reps working within this opaque industry are both hurt and helped by it. On the one hand, their job is made very difficult by virtue of the fact that they have access to only a third of the information they need to do their job the right way; on the other hand, they are not held accountable to proving whether or not they have delivered what they promised with cold, hard numbers. It is the client who is most likely to lose in this existing system—and often without ever even realizing it.

If a firm's culture already lays the foundation for trust, relationship building, and service—and commits to that foundation through transparency and accountability—there will come a time when its reputation for those things will be able to speak for it. If a client knows that they can expect a higher level customer experience while also receiving verifiable assurance that they've walked away with the best deal possible—that they can expect to *feel better*—then the standard by which they measure their experience in a traditional firm is likely to change. But it is also within the client's power to institute change. If the client knows to expect better, they will. And where the client goes, the industry will follow.

3

RISING THROUGH
THE RANKS

SERVICE, WHETHER IT IS IN MY PERSONAL OR professional life, is a value I hold to be one of the most important. In fact, the idea of being able to help people was one of the key reasons I was excited to move into this field. But now it was really bothering me that the business I believed was built on relationships and trust gave so little consideration to truly honoring those ideas and failed to put the client first. This frustration only got worse when I saw the impact that lack of service had on a company exec who had spent his entire life building a successful business founded on the core values of trust and honor (and who demonstrated those ideals by working with the same tenant rep broker for 15 years). The expression etched on his face was not one that I would soon be able to forget.

As I sat in the meeting with him, we fell into a robust dialogue about the amount of information to which reps were actually privy. He didn't believe me when I told him that, without another client in the same building, tenant rep brokers only know what the owners choose to tell us.

"So you're telling me," he challenged, "that the source of the information that allows you guys to determine whether I have a good deal or not is the information that's controlled by the *owners*? It's not based on the deals that are actually completed by brokers?"

"Yeah. That's exactly what I'm saying. The quarterly reports and other reports the public and brokers work with are based on advertised information—the information posted by the owners who want to lease the space at the highest possible rate of return. We can't even see what people are actually paying—not even the people next door. The only way we can know for sure what the cost per square footage is in a building is if we have already put another client in there. And even then, that's subject to change."

"So you can't just go look it up somewhere? No Googling?"

"Nope. It doesn't exist. We can see what the owners are asking, but we can't see what people are actually paying."

"So it's like your dirty little secret," he said with a sigh.

"Not at all. It's not a secret that this is the way the industry is run. It's just not something clients think to ask their brokers. If you were to ask your broker to show you cold, hard proof that your deal is based on the actual equivalent market rate, or whether the returns the landlord is receiving are aligned with the market, he'd probably be stumbling over his words."

"Well I have a lot of questions for him now."

The expression on his face had turned as he realized what I was saying...as he realized that something he thought he had understood for years was nothing like what he'd actually thought. I could see him trying not to think about money that could have been lost and calculating the questions he would include in the future: "What is someone else paying in this building?" "How much money is the landlord making off this deal?" "How do I know that this is a good deal?"

Seeing his reaction fired me up even more. When I was in my mid-twenties, it never occurred to me to question the existing system. I was simply trying to make a name for myself in the industry. In a way, like the executive, I had to learn the hard way too. In my role, I was still able to save my clients three to four times what they would have saved if they had entered into their lease on their own, but I felt like an idiot the first time I realized that I was essentially going into negotiations armed with little more than anecdotal evidence, my familiarity with the market, and an educated idea of what the owners would be willing to do.

Once I figured out that it was possible for me to have missed the mark on a negotiation (even one I thought was very good), I would start putting in research a few months later to test whether it was as good as I believed. There was nothing worse than finding out that the deal I had landed for a client wasn't as good as I'd thought it was. Maybe the root of the problem was that my background was in finance; I was a numbers guy who didn't care much for abstract ideas or intangible value because they didn't feel real. When I sat down to figure out how the deal the vice chairman and I had done for our client compared to the deal I had overheard, I was finally able to see tangible value—only it didn't go in the direction it should have. That value—the only hard numbers I was seeing in my role—was the 30% difference between my client's deal and the one signed by the guy next door; my client paid $1,000,000, while his client paid $750,000. So I started thinking about how it could be done better.

A lot of hours in the office, coupled with quite a bit of luck, blessed me in my career at quite an early age. I was enjoying an unprecedented level of success. I was recognized as a top-producing commercial real estate professional in Houston and was starting to get a lot of recognition inside the company and within the industry. I was named the 2012 "Rising Star" by the National Association of Industrial and Office Properties and was recognized by two different publications as a leader in the Houston real estate scene. I loved my work and was enjoying my success, but the unknown element of my job was driving me crazy. I wish I could say that I was moved to reform the industry and lead everyone into the Age of Transparency and a brighter, more lucrative future for tenant rep brokers and their clients. I'd love to say that I aspired to be the Upton Sinclair of the commercial real estate industry, muckraking and raising hell until I got people to change their ways. I wasn't. I hadn't yet come to the conclusion that there was anything beyond the individualistic way the industry operates, so I wanted to figure out a way to make this broken system work for me and to create a brighter and more lucrative future for myself.

I started by thinking about the landlords. If I was going to get the better of them, I had to get inside their heads and understand their processes. How were they making their decisions? I talked to my friends, mentors, and everyone I knew in the real estate investment business, and finally, I started to get a picture of what was really going on. What I ultimately realized was that I, and every other tenant rep broker, was simply negotiating against the market. Our biggest weapon in our negotiations with the other side was creating competition between two buildings and then using that as leverage against the landlords to try to get the best deal possible. That was how we created value for our clients. It was Negotiating 101. But the people we were negotiating against were not the sort who dabbled on introductory levels. We were missing a big piece of the puzzle. We were negotiating against sophisticated, finance-driven real estate investment trusts, insurance companies, and private equity firms. These people were smart. They were savvy. The people responsible for actually making the decisions weren't even in the room with us, and they were basing the majority of their decisions on something we weren't even thinking about. They had their own valuation and targeted rates of return that were the center of their negotiation strategy and tactics; they certainly weren't paying attention to the competition we were trying to stir up between them and another building. But I now had two of the three pieces of the puzzle—the market and the financial underwriting approach.

These behind-the-scenes decision makers were offering inflated quote rates, knowing that it was the most important metric we had available to us. The market was important to them too: If the market was increasing, it would provide leverage to the owner to increase the rate of return even further—returns that surpassed even their valuation. However, the market assumptions are just part of the information they would use to determine whether the transaction at hand met their underwriting. Grossly simplified, the "market" asking rates might be $30 per square foot, but the smart folks behind the scenes know they only need $25 to give their investors the rate of return they are obligated to per their partnership agreements. But that $5-per-square-foot savings doesn't go straight to you; it's their window for negotiation. They can come down to $28 and still exceed their actual rate of return. It helped to get an understanding of this through my I-bank real estate guys (previously mentioned) and my two new partners, who were previous landlords (and were responsible for calling the shots).

When reflecting, it was pretty stunning to think that we weren't underwriting the premises to find their rate of returns just like they were. It was even more stunning to realize that so few brokerage professionals were aware of, or had even dug into, this type of data. But as I was learning, it wasn't standard for anyone to challenge the status quo. I had a few conversations with a few "old guard" coworkers and was met with the kind of reaction I had come to expect: "The market is the market. If someone is willing to pay a certain price, then that's what sets the market."

I could understand where he was coming from. If I hadn't already seen stacks of transactions that had told me otherwise, I might have believed him. The sale of the LA Clippers is a great example of the malleable market he described. The team sold for two billion dollars. Two *billion* dollars. Are the LA Clippers worth that price? No, of course not. But there are only 30 teams in the NBA, teams come up for sale very rarely, and when they do, there is a lot of competition to drive up the price. Under those circumstances, saying "The market is the market" is accurate. Steve Ballmer wanted that team, and he was willing to overpay for it. The commercial real estate market conditions in Houston don't generate the kind of demand that actually drive prices up or down in an auction-type fashion. There are 200 million square feet of office, and in 10 years on the job, I've only ever had to compete for space once. There is always office space available. Even the residential real estate market is wildly more competitive. Commercial real estate is also missing another important component: emotional uniqueness. People can connect to a certain house. They can certainly connect to the idea of owning a basketball team. But, for the most part, the same office space can be created in many very, very similar buildings. If I can't have this office, I will go next door, lease that office over there, and be just as happy. When received, the space is essentially an empty canvas that can be constructed in any way one can imagine based on a multitude of needs and the budget. There is rarely a need for a tenant to compete for office space, and "the market is the market" rings hollow without any competition to make the statement true.

I realized that if I was going to negotiate the best deal possible for my client—without later finding out that I could have done better—I had to start playing the game that the owners and landlords were playing. I had to learn how to value a building the same way they did.

I fell back on a combination of my entry-level analyst experience and the happy-hour conversations with my I-banking friends to find my answer.

There may not have been a central database pertaining to the market value of every commercial real estate space in Houston—no way of knowing how much the properties were actually leasing for—but surely, there was *some* information out there that I could find. When was the building sold? For how much? What is the debt package of the building? What is the current NOI on the building? How much did they spend on capital improvements? There must have been some other way to figure out what the other side was taking in consideration while making their deals. The real estate investment banking side is responsible for valuing these buildings in the event that the owner decides to sell. This information is kept confidential by the owners and landlords, of course, but at some point, it all has to come together so they can go market their building to sell it.

I pored over the available information until I was able to find something I could use (in the vast majority of commercial office buildings, I could find some if not all the information). From that, I could ascertain the amount of money landlords were making on their deals, and then I could take it a step further and extrapolate the rate of return desired by the companies leasing the space. Those latent finance skills I picked up in college, during all the happy-hour discussions with my investment friends, and even the hours I spent in the copy room as an analyst had paid off in a way I never would have expected.

I realized fairly quickly that we had it all wrong. The owners and landlords weren't basing their decisions solely on the state of the commercial real estate market; they were making decisions, within a bandwidth, based on whether they were hitting the underwriting in their analyses and what effect that would have on their exit strategy when it came time to sell. Everything we were doing to create huge inefficiencies in the market was doing little more than impacting the advertised asking price. But there were other factors: It may equate to the talent or experience of the broker, whether the landlord believed there truly was competition, whether they were playing a numbers game in which 75% of all current tenants would renew and 40% of all prospective new tenants would sign despite the rate, or whether they knew the executives lived nearby; it could even come down to whether they respected the broker. When it came to the other side's actual decision making, we weren't moving the needle. I had to figure out their numbers—the things they were actually using to determine their decisions—if I was going to successfully negotiate against them. If we sat back down at the proverbial poker table, I wanted to be able to see their hand.

I combed back through old deals. I pulled numbers from previous leases, cross-referenced them against the landlords' financial information, and then estimated the desired rate of return. Through a lot of conversations with developers, REIT managers, and our real estate investment bank and capital markets teammates, I was finally able to figure out what kind of threshold the companies on the other side of the table were allowed to work within; I figured out where they wanted to be, and more importantly, I figured out how low they were allowed to go. I found where they measured their point of indifference and how much they were willing to take the risk of having to find another prospective tenant.

As an example (and in more simplistic terms), I may be able to easily calculate that a REIT may be quoting a rate that yields a 17% unleveraged cash-on-cash yield but underwrote the investment of 10%–11% on the particular building we were negotiating. If all a broker has is the ability to create competition from the market as negotiating leverage, oftentimes not knowing if the competitive set is as low as possible, in that way, they are negotiating blind. But with this new clarity in how the process works, I felt like I could see their bandwidth and my negotiating room. I may not get them all the way down to 10%, thanks to factors such as creditworthiness, but I could push them to the bottom of their bandwidth.

And it worked.

As the rate of successful deals, all of which were now backed by hard numbers, climbed, I was able to deliver this message to my clients. My personal stock in the company and within the industry started rising steadily. I soared through the ranks, and at 25, I became the youngest director in my company's history. I was also feeling far more satisfied with the service I was providing to my clients, because I was able to give them more than just my opinion. I had carved out a little slice of transparency in an opaque market, and it was benefiting my clients and my career greatly. I started to realize that within this system of individual entrepreneurs, there were other people (and companies) pushing for transparency based on data and information sharing. In fact, the idea was being pursued and implemented by some of the largest and most impressive firms in the world. If I had, I might have gone looking for them. Instead, they found me.

4

CHANGE WON'T
BE EASY

THE TENANT REP INDUSTRY AS IT STANDS WON'T suddenly go away. The fact is, as long as companies are operating and functioning collectively, there will be a need for tenant rep brokers. Even with rental rate discrepancies, the benefit to the client far outweighs anything they could negotiate for themselves. Even in an opaque market, the broker has (and is) leverage in the negotiations with owners and landlords. Tenant reps are so necessary and are still capable of negotiating a lease down to multiples better than tenants doing it themselves. The fact is, introducing the transparency, accountability, and service-oriented perspective that I believe the commercial real estate industry desperately needs is no easy task. The building owners and landlords who benefit so much from the existing opaque system are not about to let that change without a fight. And traditional tenant reps—those individual entrepreneurs—are reticent to endure the short-term pain that comes with shifting to a culture of collaboration, information sharing, and transparency. It would level the playing field internally at brokerage shops. This shift is made even more difficult by the fact that it requires a complete overhaul of the existing system; small tweaks and changes won't be effective as long as firms remain on a sales model.

These are the obstacles that stand in the way of challenging the status quo. But that doesn't mean that it can't be done. In fact, the firm that approached me—the world's largest commercial real estate group and a firm that has been around for years—was leading the charge to do just that. They were overhauling the way that they did business, bucking "the way things are done" for a truly client-first model.

They were implementing a new information-sharing platform, starting at the highest level. They were forcing all information to be shared and all work to be collaborative from the top down. They were hiring managing directors for each office—unbiased people put in place to build a company culture that, up until that moment, had been unheard of in the commercial real estate industry. This firm recognized the same need for transparency that I did, but they were actually big enough to make it happen. They were willing to put up with some initial discomfort in order to set the company on a new track. I couldn't imagine how they were making it work and could only guess what that "initial discomfort" actually looked like. This was the first I had heard of a company "breaking the mold" in this old school business.

Unfortunately, this "discomfort" is something that very few commercial real estate firms (and the professionals within them) are willing to endure. And when a firm's highest producer is willing to leverage his position to keep things the way they are, it presents a huge obstacle to change.

Just as a superstar basketball player is able to throw his influence around in the offices of his team's organization, so too are a commercial real estate firm's heavy producers—the guys who produce significant revenue. In the same way that LeBron James gets to weigh in on closed-door issues, these producers get to have their say when it comes to making major decisions, such as whether the existing system that has served them so well should remain unexamined. If you were to walk into the offices of many tenant reps in Houston, Texas and say, "Hey, you're going to have to take on some short-term pain, and you're going to have to share your information, but it will be for the long-term benefit of our clients and the company," you would be met with a resounding NO. The heavy producers, the guys making 10 to 15 million dollars a year in the individualist business, have no interest in sharing the personal experience and privileged information that has put them at the highest level. Why would they? It's at the core of what they have spent their career and lives building.

These producers have the leverage to look out for their personal interests and have the ability to convince their companies to maintain the status quo, and they're not afraid to use it. In most cases, if the CEO of a traditional firm were to decide to move forward with a new, transparent, information-sharing system anyway, it would be with the very high risk of his producers walking away—and that's enough to end the discussion. Most firms are not willing to support that kind of earning capital just walking out the door. One of the more well-known commercial real estate firms in Houston is a $50 million office. If their $15 million producer walks away, the office is closed. It's simply not an option for them. Very few companies are committed enough to transparency and accountability to risk the defection of their biggest players.

Those producers are willing to walk away because, to them, sharing their information is akin to giving away all their trade secrets. In the individualized nature of this business, in which the rep *is the commodity*, making the decision to contribute to a shared database is akin to setting a pile of money on fire. Collaboration flies in the face of the long-held industry culture. This idea was perfectly summed up by one of the biggest producers in the Houston market. He reflected on his success for a newspaper article: "Early on I learned not to talk about my business, even with my friends." When professionals have built their career on a certain way of thinking, it is no small task to convince them to start thinking another way, especially when walking out the door is an option.

Yet, without the buy-in and contribution of every member of the firm, an internal database can't work. *Everyone* has to contribute their information in the name of transparency. *Everyone* has to be willing to take on some short-term discomfort. And that is a big ask.

When this new firm's management was recruiting me, they kept referring to an internal database that resembled an MLS (multiple listing service—another nonexistent term in the commercial real estate tenant rep industry) and using terms such as "managed brokerage," to which I replied that I didn't want to be managed by anyone. I was so entrenched in the traditional system that I didn't even know what they were really saying. Then, when it finally clicked that they had created a system built on a collaborative effort to make sure the client was getting served first, I didn't believe them.

But as we kept talking, I got more and more excited. The theory of what they were doing intrigued me. The idea of collaborating within a client-first model, rather than working individually within a sales model, sounded amazing. I wouldn't have to hide or protect my information when I was chasing a piece of business. My coworkers could be my *coworkers* instead of my *competition*. At my current firm, it was common to realize that the guy at the next desk was a better fit for your client's needs and then never mention it to either of them. Why let your client get away just because it's a better move for them? Under this new firm's system, I would have an unbiased managing director saying, "No, you and you are going to go work on this deal together."

Then there was the internal database itself. The idea of being able to work within a platform in which information was actually shared and I would be able to show it to a client—"Hey, here's what other tenants are paying"—was intriguing. I was especially interested in their database, but I wasn't entirely sure that it would work—or that it even could work— well enough to be trusted in my own negotiations. Is everyone contributing? After everything I had done to build my own system, I wasn't about to risk turning my deals back over to "good guessing."

In order for the information in the internal database to be 100% unequivocally good, they needed everybody's buy-in, and based on what I had seen and in my experience, it was no easy feat to convince the most senior producers to give up the goods when that meant taking money out of their pockets. Still, the new firm and its dedication to transparency was so much more in line with what I believed was best for the industry. It was their dedication that led me to believe that I had found the missing component—the final third of the puzzle that would lend me a full view of my opponent's poker hand. Could I afford to pass up on the opportunity? But there was another, nagging question: Could I afford to take it?

5

WALKING AWAY

I WAS VERY FORTUNATE IN MY CURRENT position, and there was every reason to believe that I had enormous growth opportunity—that I was being primed for huge success and a high ceiling. In other words, there were a lot of good reasons to stay where I was. Still, I couldn't shake the idea of working within a client-first model. I liked the ethics that were the cornerstone of what this other firm was doing. It felt like what the future of the industry should be. And that's when I began weighing the short-term benefits of staying where I was against my long-term career. The short term didn't concern me much, but I was worried about what the next 30 years would look like if I stayed.

When I left my role at my old firm, everyone around me was floored. They couldn't understand why I would choose to walk away when my upward trajectory in that office was unimpeded. They were even more confused when I told them about the company's new policies. The way some of them looked at me, you would have thought I was relinquishing all of my possessions and moving to a remote monastery.

When I got to my new role, the first thing I did was dive into their central database. I was a man on a mission, and I knew exactly what I was looking for.

A few months prior, I had executed a deal at the same time and in the same building as another vice chairman with the company. This guy was old guard, had been a producer for decades, and had the swagger to match. He certainly wasn't intimidated by our parallel negotiations, and he was going to make sure I knew that. He walked over to my desk with a huge smile on his face and said, "I took the landlord to the mat on this deal."

Immediately, I started to think about my own deal: $20 per square foot. I had felt good about it. I had known in advance how much the building had been purchased for and had used my financial model to drive the deal. I trusted my system, of course, but this guy was one of our biggest producers. He brought in millions and millions of dollars each year. He was also representing a much more attractive client than I was; the company he was representing needed 35,000 square feet, which would make their deal much more valuable to the landlord and would typically warrant them more leverage (and thus a lower rent) than my 10,000 square foot-seeking clients. And he was sitting on my desk like he owned it.

"How'd you do?" I asked him.

"I got a $24 deal. How about you?"

In my mind, I was thinking, "Holy *&$@!" A $4 per square foot difference meant that his client had over-paid by roughly $800,000! In a direct comparison of rental rates, the deal I had negotiated was more than 25% more financially advantageous. I replied with "Twenty" and hoped it didn't come off as smug.

His eyes narrowed. "What the hell? Why weren't we talking during the deal? Why didn't I know about this?"

"I don't know," was the only answer I had for him.

Now I was looking for that building in the firm's database to confirm whether the vice chairman could have negotiated the same rate for his deal. My suspicions were confirmed almost immediately. The firm's data was up to date, it was totally sound, and it would have saved this guy's client a lot of money if information sharing had been a part of the culture at my old firm.

Then I looked up another building—one I had been helping a coworker in negotiations with just as I'd left. Admittedly, I thought we had done a pretty good job. He thought he had negotiated an amazing deal. In fact, he'd been so sure about it that he'd convinced his client to extend their term by a few extra years. Now I was going to find out if we'd been right.

I clicked through the central database to find the building and all related transactions. I scrolled through until—

"Dammit!"

Unfortunately for our client, we'd been wrong. The deal hadn't been nearly as good as we'd thought it had been. The firm had recently done a deal in the same building with a smaller company for $2 per square foot less than we had done. The discrepancy—our wrong guess—had cost our client a million dollars.

Worse, our confidence in our interpretation and subsequent negotiation had convinced the clients to lock themselves into a longer lease at that rate. If I had never looked, we would have never thought it was anything less than an amazing deal.

6

DEBUNKING MYTHS

I WALKED AWAY FROM THE FIRM IN WHICH I had built my career—where I was the youngest director in the company's history and was receiving numerous honors as one of the top brokers in the industry—for a role with a company that I felt could move the industry in the right direction. My goal now is to marry my individual approach to benchmarking the other side's rate of returns to create a clear, true overview of the market that brings their tactics into the daylight and levels the playing field. But with resistance coming from all sides, change is not going to be easy.

Introducing transparency into the commercial real estate market is not a small fix. There is no Band-Aid that will make the industry more favorable to clients, thereby reducing the need for major reform. Transparency will change everything; the market will become an entirely new thing. I want this change to happen, and I truly believe that the industry will eventually move in this direction. I want to help lead the way. The first step in introducing the huge shift in perspective this industry needs begins with debunking some myths.

The story of David and Goliath is the age-old tale of the young guy who faced a giant with nothing but a slingshot to help him. David fires a masterful shot, kills the giant, and becomes king—a classic underdog story.

In *David and Goliath: Underdogs, Misfits, and the Art of Battling Giants*, Malcolm Gladwell suggests an entirely different perspective on this well-known story and the presumed advantage and disadvantage of the two title characters. In Gladwell's retelling, Goliath isn't a crazed giant who is hell-bent on destroying the town and every last one of its citizens. He's sick with acromegaly—specifically, a disease that causes the body to produce excess growth hormone. His size and disfigurement are due to a physical condition over which he has no control. His disease also impacts his eyesight, making it difficult for Goliath to see even a few feet past his face. All of these add up to a guy who is great at terrifying the townspeople but not necessarily someone who can easily win a fight, especially when the other guy is well armed.

Gladwell also explains that slingshots were genuine weapons back then—not the toy that Dennis the Menace types like to carry around. The rock coming from David's slingshot could produce the equivalent stopping power of a bullet shot out of a .45 caliber pistol; this thing was a gun—not a toy. It could do some serious damage, especially in the hands of someone with really great accuracy, which David had. Already, the underdog narrative is upended. David isn't an underdog at all. You've got a lumbering, sick guy who can't see very well against a marksman armed with a .45.

It's not like David swung a rock and got lucky. The story means something very different today than it did back when people *fought* with slingshots, because our perception of the events are very different. We are presuming Goliath's advantage because we know he is big, but we never think to look for the reason behind his size: Why is Goliath big? Does that actually mean he is more powerful? Similarly, we assume David's disadvantage because he has only a slingshot, and our idea of what that means is rooted in old Dennis the Menace reruns, so we don't realize that we've skipped over some crucial information: What exactly can that slingshot do? What kind of damage is it capable of?

"We have a definition in our heads of what an advantage is," Gladwell says. He goes on to state:

> *The definition isn't right. And what happens as a result? It means that we make mistakes. It means that we misread battles between underdogs and giants. It means that we underestimate how much freedom there can be in what looks like a disadvantage.*

This is exactly what is happening in the tenant rep industry. When customers are choosing representation, the easy assumption is that the older execs—the Goliaths of the industry—are the strongest choice. The old guard and the time-tested, unquestioned way of doing business offers a level of stability that can be appealing and easy to trust. People assume that it's very advantageous to hire someone who has been in the business for 30 years, but they never think to ask an important question: What if it's 30 years of experience doing the wrong thing?

The presumed advantage is in the eyes of the client.

They see these Goliaths as unbeatable, but time and time again, I see these same giants fall when it comes to actual numbers. It isn't that these reps are doing a bad job—most of them are very, very good at what they do—it's that the way they do their job doesn't work anymore. The markets have continued to change, while their system has remained the same.

Experience is valuable, of course, but to presume that it's the number one marker for success is to misread the battle.

Experience can also mean that a tenant rep in the traditional system is very set in his ways, especially when there has been little demand for him to change or even an indication that he needs to. Again, because of the way the system works, most tenant reps have no way of knowing for sure that they scored the best deal for their client. Therefore, there's no way to measure the effectiveness of what they're doing. To quote again, "You can't manage what you can't measure." It's a line that's been around almost as long as the story of David and Goliath...and with good reason. If you don't measure something, there is no way to know if it's doing better or worse over time; and if you *choose* not to measure something, I think it's because you either don't value it, or you don't want to have to change it.

If a client is about to sign a multimillion-dollar lease, and they trust their tenant rep to oversee and manage the transaction, they presume that the rep is basing their negotiation on a stack of objective measurements. That simply isn't the case. The measurables that most traditional firms rely on are based on insignificant or nonexistent information. Subjective measurement offers little in the way of constructive feedback, which means traditional firms don't have to face a need for change. Why change if no one is making you?

This is how you end up with dinosaurs, long-standing traditional firms, and the big producers that reside in them. They have very little competition, internal or external, because they've been around forever and are an established name in the industry. These are the guys who clients assume have the biggest advantage in negotiations, so they flock to them cash in hand. These are also the guys who have absolutely zero incentive to change the way they do business. It's not even a consideration.

When I left my old firm, the guys sitting at the top of the company had no idea why. They asked, "What do we need to do? What do we need to change?" I tried to explain my desire to work within a new, transparent system. I told them about the free sharing of information and collaboration that is a cornerstone of my new firm's culture. But as they began to examine what a similar shift would look like on their individual level, the talks began to falter. What would they *personally* gain by moving toward transparency? They were so set in their ways and had benefited so much from the individualized system that they had little interest in shaking up the status quo.

Another myth that needs to come into question is whether the sales model on which the tenant rep industry is built is the most effective. As we saw with the Adobe Grand Villas, a client-first model can do wonders for building a company's reputation and raising the customer's standard of expected service. I would argue that the existing sales model with a client-first model would elevate the commercial real estate industry as a whole, perhaps giving us all more incentive to increase transparency on the tenant rep side, to share information, collaborate, and do whatever it takes to deliver on the promises we make to our clients.

But that isn't what happens in most firms. Instead, the sales model dictates that the rep is the commodity and upholds the individualized nature of the role that stands solidly in the way of making this necessary change. Most businesses have an account manager, a salesperson, and a finance person, all being actual experts with years of experience in their respective fields. Under a transparent system, a tenant rep firm would have to do the same thing: We would have to have actual experts in place to do the things that require an expert's eye. Real experts, however, are more expensive and require an upfront investment, which makes it easier for those at the top to sweep the problem under the rug. Rather than change the system, most traditional firms opt to spin their wheels. They prefer to hire cold callers instead. The fact is, it's easier to maintain the status quo than it is to make a company-wide move toward transparency. Some of the leading companies in the world, however, are doing just that.

The tenant rep business is so sales oriented that one of its primary business development methods comes directly out of the sales model playbook—cold calling. In a particularly good market, like we have now, companies are hiring more and more cold callers. They've got a room of 23-year-olds churning through the phones; it's like *Boiler Room* come to life. In an industry that is supposed to be built on relationships and trust, these cold callers are creating nothing but noise—"I can save you money on your real estate lease!" These messages are flooding the phones and email boxes of anyone who is renting commercial space, so much so that their reaction is mostly to dig their heels in the sand. I've spoken to tenants who I know are in a bad situation with their lease, but they are so inundated by people promising to "show them a better way" that their response is immediate: "I've had a broker for ten years. Leave me alone." When clients are busy enough with their own work in their own industry, they are not about to take the time to explore finding a new broker if they're relatively happy with the one they've got. The noise generated by these cold callers increases the hassle, which, in turn, makes it more likely that the clients will entrench themselves where they are and never even realize that there is truly an alternative way of doing business out there. The client's standard of expectation never changes, and things stay the way they are.

The idea that cold calling and other sales tactics are the best way to run the tenant rep industry is another myth that needs to be taken down.

The final myth is that the industry will never change. "The way things are" isn't the way they *have* to be. The landscape of the industry will change. It just requires a few companies, reps, and clients to make the commitment to usher in this change by changing the culture to one of transparency and accountability, raising the standard of service, and raising the standard of expectation, even if it means weathering a little discomfort. I truly believe that even a handful of those who are willing can effect an industry-wide change.

Tony Hsieh knows this better than anyone. He was an entrepreneur and investor who already had two successful companies under his belt when his friend, Nick Swinmurn, approached him in 1999 with the idea to start selling shoes online. Hsieh almost disregarded the idea entirely. After all, why would people want to buy shoes if they couldn't try them on beforehand? Swinmurn changed his mind when he told Hsieh that 5% of the $40 billion market was already being sold through mail-order catalogs. Hsieh was won over and invested $2 million into ShoeSite, which would eventually become Zappos. In 2000, Hsieh joined Swinmurn as co-CEO of the company.

Hsieh said, "I wanted to have a whole company built around [customer service]," and he followed through with this desire. He and Swinmurn built Zappos on a loyalty business model that is so good that you couldn't get a customer service rep to tell you "no" even if you tried. Customers responded, and they did so quickly. In his first year at Zappos, the company brought in $1.6 million in revenue; 2001 brought in $8.6 million; and by 2008, Zappos hit $1 billion in annual sales. In doing so, they also changed the customer's perspective on 1) buying shoes outside of a shoe store and 2) receiving an extraordinary level of customer service that rivaled any offline business. Hsieh raised his customers' standard of expectation and won their trust at a time when people were still skeptical of online shopping. Zappos has an impressive 75% repeat customer rate, and where the customers went, the industry followed.

But changing the landscape of the industry (and customer expectations) wasn't easy, nor was it without discomfort. To better their customer service, Hsieh opted to move away from their old shipping model, in which manufacturers shipped the shoes directly to the customer, in favor of expanding their warehouse by 77,000 feet in order to control every stage of the customer experience. Losing the "drop shipping" meant an immediate 25% drop in revenue all at once while taking on a massive new commercial space. "Uncomfortable" is an understatement. In an interview with INC Magazine, Hsieh said about that time, "We thought about going under every day." The short-term sacrifice paid off as Zappos grew 948% in three years.

Tony Hsieh was willing to give up short-term gains and personal comfort for the sake of building a better company. He was willing to sacrifice those things to do the right thing for his customers and do them the right way. His perspective is one that I admire. Similarly, I admired my company leadership's willingness to tell their producers flat out, "This new, shared information system is not optional. We want you to stay with us, but we understand if you choose to go," even if it meant losing some of their biggest guys. Did they let a lot of money walk out the door as some of these producers defected? Of course. But they chose to withstand the loss and move forward. This is what I want to see more of the traditional firms do and what I truly believe will be the first step to reshaping the industry.

As tenant rep brokers, we can begin to effect this change by showing our existing and potential clients that they can expect more from us. By raising the standard of our service, we raise our customers' expectations of what they *should* be getting from their tenant rep broker—verifiable numbers, actual expertise, and a business model that puts them before the bottom line. If their current tenant rep broker won't provide them with that, perhaps they'll go find another rep at another firm who will. And when enough traditional firms lose enough clients to that higher standard of service, those firms might just come around too. As brokerage firms begin to shift over to this new, transparent, collaborative model, perhaps the industry standard of information sharing will begin to shift too, extending to expanded MLS systems and best practices. Slowly but surely, the tenant rep industry would continue to shed light on the opaque commercial real estate market—all 200 million square feet of it—until we could sit across the table from the owners and landlords and know exactly what we were dealing with. No manipulations. No educated guesses. Just a transparent market that operates fairly for both sides. This is the change I am working for.

This is the change that our clients have the power to make too. They must realize that they have a choice in the type of firm they do business with and that their choice is very important in determining the future of the industry. I believe the perfect example of this can be derived from a Wall Street scandal.

"They know a little bit and they trust that the market works. And that trust has been broken. The market should just be a neutral place that buyers and sellers can meet—almost like a referee." My ears perked up as Brad Katsuyama spoke about the misplaced faith investors were putting into the fairness they believed existed in the stock markets and described what he believed the market ought to look like. If I had read what he'd said out of context, I would have believed he was talking about the state of commercial real estate brokerage and the clients who put too much faith in its broken system.

I had first learned about Katsuyama's story through *Flash Boys*, the book by Michael Lewis that tells the story of how Brad, then a trader with Royal Bank of Canada, uncovered secret and systemic abuse of the trading systems on Wall Street and chose to walk away from a lucrative job to start his own exchange built on the transparency and fairness he felt was missing in the market.

Immediately, I felt I could relate to his story.

As Katsuyama would place large orders, he kept noticing that his trades didn't go through. Instead, he would have to re-place the order, which was now listed at a slightly higher price. After digging around, doing tons of research, and questioning a bunch of different experts, he figured out that the problem stemmed from the high-frequency trading (HFT) that was happening in mysterious "dark pools." The activity wasn't illegal; in fact, it was happening so quickly that most people didn't even know it was happening. But this "front running" was taking a ton of money out of the pockets of ordinary traders and major investment firms alike, scamming millions of dollars under the cover of an opaque submarket. With the help of a team of experts and "puzzle masters," Katsuyama was able to determine that it was the speed with which the orders could reach the exchanges that was allowing HFT traders to front-run investors. Simply put, they had faster fiber optics, and this gave them a few extra microseconds with which they could buy and resell the stock at a higher price.

Even when he blew the whistle on HFT, very few of the big investment firms, including RBC, opted to change their ways. It would have meant sacrificing short-term gains to change a system from which they were already benefiting. Frustrated, Brad opted to leave his lucrative job to create his own exchange, IEX, which was predicated on a model that prioritized transparency and fairness. Inside his office, Katsuyama has a box that contains 60km of fiber optic wiring, enough to slow down all trades coming into IEX enough to make front running impossible. When *60 Minutes* sat him down to ask him why he made his decision to walk away from a comfortable role and a high paycheck to start something new, he responded: "Well, I wanted to be able to provide something that was transparent." He believed it was the right thing to do, so he did it.

IEX got off to a slow start but now handles 58 million trades a day. Now that word has gotten out about the market manipulation happening in dark pools, the promise of fairness and transparency at IEX is a major motivator behind their upswing. It took time, but now Brad Katsuyama is making the difference he hoped to make: He's offering people a choice. But first he had to show them why their choice was important.

Our clients have a choice too, and their choice is important. As a client, you have a choice. You can raise your standard of expectation for the tenant rep service you receive. And you can ask questions:

How do I know I got a good deal?

Why don't we know how much money the landlord is making off this deal?

Why don't we know how much the other tenant on this floor is paying?

As a client, you deserve to have all the information available to you, to *know* that you got the best deal possible, and to feel assured that you aren't paying a million dollars more than your neighbor. You deserve to *feel better*. The choice is yours to make.

This is my goal for my career, for my company, and for my industry. The industry will shift. I truly believe that. This won't be a quick fix. After all, it requires an entire overhaul of the existing system. It's just going to take some time before transparency, collaboration, and service work their way into tenant rep methodology. I'm not the only person that's calling this out, but it's a difficult thing to cut through the noise of cold callers, critics, and those who benefit too much from the status quo to want it to change. There are a few firms leading the charge, but I have no doubt that other companies will open their eyes to how this business is manipulated and decide to make a change, even if that change is uncomfortable at first. Tenant rep brokers have a choice—shift their perspectives and reorient their business in a way that puts clients before their bottom line and collaboration over individual interest or wait until they are forced to. Change will come, but as Brad Katsuyama said, "It takes time to convince people to do something differently."

www.ingramcontent.com/pod-product-compliance
Lightning Source LLC
Chambersburg PA
CBHW070944210326
41520CB00021B/7041